AFTER THE

THE RECONSTRUCTION OF EVANGELICALISM

DAVID N. SAMUEL

General Secretary of the Protestant Reformation Society

THE HARRISON TRUST

1980

An address given to the Annual Meeting of the Blackburn Diocesan Evangelical Union, October, 1979.

Published for the Protestant Reformation Society
by The Harrison Trust
East Ravendale Rectory
Grimsby, South Humberside, DN37 0RX.

1 SBN 0 907223 00 1

AFTER THE FIRE

"A sudden fierce gust of wind took all who were at the ceremony completely by surprise. Hats were blown off and copies of the Vicar's speech and other rubbish were scattered over the site" (Local newspaper report). There are undoubtedly those, though not I trust here, who will regard what I have to say tonight as rubbish, and old rubbish, because it relates to the past and to the controversies of the past. A friend of mine, who is a student at one of our theological colleges, made some passing reference in discussion to the Reformation, to which the response was, 'But that was a long time ago'. In that way we cut ourselves off from our heritage and our roots, and leave ourselves with no sense of direction. I have been struck by how many of Bishop Ryle's books have titles with the word 'old' in them: *Old Paths* and *Light from Old Times*, for example. But Bishop Ryle was not irrelevant. His message impinged only too sharply for many upon the times in which he lived. And so it is a fallacy of shallow thinking to dismiss what happened long ago as irrelevant. What is true is not new, or as Karl Barth once put it, 'What was once of grave importance is so still'.

Long, long ago the truth was found
A company of men it bound
Grasp firmly then – that ancient truth.

But you will notice that this affectation to despise the past is selective. Men despise the truths of the Reformation, because they say they are old, but the hoary errors of the Church of Rome and of pagan philosophy, tricked out in the garb of modern religion and modern thought they readily embrace as dynamic, exciting, and relevant. Such is the spirit of the age, but such has been the spirit of every age. The important thing is that we see through it and are not led astray by it.

I come now to my subject which is divided into three parts. First, What is Evangelicalism? Secondly, What are its relations to be with other groupings within, and outside, the Church of England? And thirdly, What is its role to be in the future?

First, *What is Evangelicalism?* The word 'evangel' means gospel, and evangelicalism means that system of doctrine which is expressive of the Gospel. The word relates primarily to doctrine. This is the distinctive feature of evangelicalism which sets it apart from other groupings in the church. Our doctrines are those things by which we are distinguished, and by which, we believe, the Gospel is distinguished from that which often passes for it.

It is well to be clear about this, for there are those who think that to be an evangelical is to be someone who lays claim to a certain kind of experience. It surely goes without saying that a true evangelical is a converted man, but this is not the distinctive mark of the position that he holds. He is distinguished from others by his teaching not his experience. If we do not keep this before us we shall get very confused. There are very many other people, besides evangelicals, who lay claim to some experience. There are the charismatic Christians who say their lives have been wonderfully transformed by an experience of God, but this does not make them evangelicals, because many of them have no clear idea of what teachings they hold, and others adhere to systems which are the very antithesis of evangelicalism. So experience cannot be the criterion. It is because some evangelicals thought it to be so, and in consequence turned evangelicalism into pietism, that we are in the situation we are in today. It is one of the reasons why there is so much confusion between charismatics and neo-evangelicals, and why the one seems so much like the other. This is where we need the light from old times. The Reformers were faced with a similar situation. The Spirituals and Anabaptists at the time of the Reformation were men who professed an experience and inward illumination, but the Reformers were in no doubt about the difference between themselves and these men. They did not adhere to the distinctive teachings of evangelicalism. That was the difference, and it was sufficient to preserve the integrity of the Reformation.

Evangelicalism is, then, distinguished by its doctrines; it is these that give it its peculiar character, and it is by adherence to them that a man is known as an evangelical. What are these teachings? They can be summarized very simply from the XXXIX Articles. The primacy and authority of Scripture and its sufficiency for salvation. The depravity and sinfulness of man's nature, so that he can do nothing worthy of salvation. The perfect sacrifice and oblation of Christ upon the cross, which needs nothing added to it, so that the mere suggestion of a supplementary or complementary work of man is blasphemy. The justification of the sinner by the imputed righteousness of Christ, through faith alone. The need for worthy reception of the sacraments of Baptism and the Lord's Supper by true repentance and lively faith in the promises of God in the Gospel. The spiritual presence of Christ in the heart of the believer, not in the bread and wine of the sacrament.

Now all these things are not separate and discrete teachings so that you are at liberty to accept this and reject that. They are all of a piece. One logically entails another, so that once you start you are obliged to accept them all, because they all belong together and cohere in one systematic body of teaching. Furthermore they are all derived from the plain teaching of the Bible. When the word of God is received in an honest and good heart, these teachings impress themselves unmistakably upon the mind as the only possible meaning of Scripture.

In recent years some dissatisfaction has been voiced with this position amongst evangelicals. They have said, 'If all this is so plain in Scripture, why do we need the XXXIX Articles and the Book of Common Prayer to preserve them for us? Just give people the Bible and they can discover it for themselves. Let us as evangelicals simply retain the Bible and dispense with the Articles. After all, the Reformers did not possess the Articles at first.' There are two answers to that, one from commonsense and the other from history, and sometimes one is led to believe that neo-evangelicals have dispensed not only with the latter, but the former as well.

First the answer from commonsense. It would be possible I suppose for every generation to discover for itself the wheel, since it is something of such obvious necessity and utility, and nothing else can take its place. It is almost a truth of reason and if mankind did lose sight of it, it would have to be invented again, indeed, would be invented again. But why should people be left to discover this for themselves when we can pass on such knowledge to them in a very convenient way. Likewise, why should not the teachings of the Bible be expressed in a form, both systematic and concise, for the instruction of successive generations. If they accept them, they only do so because they find them to encapsulate what is the teaching of Scripture itself, and can prove it to be so for themselves.

Secondly, the answer from history. One of the greatest English Reformers was Tyndale. He was the translator *par excellence* of the Bible into English. But it did not take him long to realize that people needed not only the Bible in English, but what he called 'a pathway into Scripture', i.e., an introduction to the teachings of the Bible, so that they would be helped to recognise its great themes and teachings. Hence his many valuable introductions to the books of the Bible, which helped people to discover for themselves what were its principal doctrines. But more than this Tyndale also realized that the people needed preachers of these great teachings of the Bible, men who would set forth the doctrines of Scripture in a plain, clear, and systematic way. Hence his prayer, 'The Lord of all mercy send us preachers with power; that is to say, true expounders of the word of God. . .' How important this is. The ministry is God's gift to the church. It is to be used with the Bible. Preaching is the ordinance of God for salvation. It is the business of the preacher to understand what Scripture teaches and to set it forth plainly.

We cannot, then, under any circumstances dispense with the formulation of the distinctive doctrines of evangelicalism. It is a prime necessity for the church and the Christian. The attempt to separate the Bible from the formulation of evangelical doctrine in the XXXIX Articles, without putting anything comparable in its place, must be resisted at all costs.

Now it was about the time, in my own spiritual pilgrimage, that I was beginning to see these things for myself and accept them that I remember a significant change was beginning to come about in Anglican evangelicalism. A leading evangelical put it thus, at a meeting I attended in 1965. The time had come, he said, for evangelicals to change their stance. The old position of maintaining that evangelicalism represented the true teaching of the Church of England was no longer tenable. The ground for it had been taken away by revision of the Canons and other changes. The law was no longer on our side. New services were about to be introduced and ecumenism was growing. Adherence by evangelicals to the Book of Common Prayer and the XXXIX Articles would condemn them to irrelevancy. The situation was changing rapidly and evangelicals must be prepared to travel light. We have the Bible and that is enough.

So you see, my experience was like that of Sinbad the Sailor. You remember the story of how Sinbad and his companions one day spotted an island. They drew near the shore and disembarked. Just as they had decamped and were disporting themselves, the island began to disappear beneath them into the sea. It seems that it was no island at all, but the back of a whale. No sooner had I arrived at my theological destination, and had come to the conclusion that evangelicalism was a coherent body of doctrine derived from Scripture and crystallized in the teaching of the Reformers, than the ground began to shudder and disappear beneath my feet. Evangelicals were preparing to consign the XXXIX Articles and the Book of Common Prayer, not to the flames, but to history, henceforth to be little more than curiosities for those who had a taste for the past.

It was John Henry Newman who said that 'religion cannot maintain itself at all without theology'.* He spoke truly. He was wrong about many things, but he was right about that. The present predicament of evangelicalism is proof of that.

* *An Essay in Aid of a Grammar of Assent* (Fourth edition), 92.

The present spiritual malaise of the Church of England is proof of that. In turning our backs upon Reformation teaching we have created a theological vacuum – we have put nothing in the place of that teaching, for the simple reason that nothing can take its place. Evangelicalism stands or falls by its acceptance or rejection of those great doctrines. The Church of England stands or falls by the acceptance or rejection of those great doctrines, for they are of its essence. And so we have brought ourselves into our present unsatisfactory position of uncertainty and confusion. The remedy is obvious. If we want to see not merely evangelicalism restored, but the Church of England, we must dedicate ourselves to *the rehabilitation of the English Reformation in the English Church* in this generation. That is our goal. We must have a single eye, and theology must be paramount. The English Church and nation have for too long been alienated from their heritage by the defection of many clergy in the last century and the failure of a great number in this. We must not fail now.

This brings me to the second thing. *What are our relations to be with other groupings, for example, with Anglo-catholics within the Church of England and Roman Catholics outside?* Or, for that matter, with any other group or denomination?

The first essential in this matter of relationships is that we should know where we ourselves are going, what is our goal, our objective. We must, first, know where we are going before we can decide whether, and how, we can work with other people. If they are going in our direction, then we can go with them, but not if they are going the other way. You remember those words in the Second Book of Kings, "Is thine heart right, as my heart is with thy heart? . . . If it be, give me thine hand". We can work with any who are seeking the rehabilitation of the English Reformation in the Church of England. That is our great objective. We can go with any who are going that way.

So much that is going on in the church today militates against that principle. Why then should we be expected to fall in with it? The reasoning is rather like this. You are going to Edinburgh and I am going to London. Well, then, we shall split the difference and go to Manchester. But why should I go to Manchester? I have no business in Manchester. My business is in London. It's all right to agree to go to Manchester if you have got nothing to do, and nowhere in particular to go!

This is what is going on in the church today. It is the process of consensus-seeking. Everybody must arrive at agreement with everybody else by splitting the difference. Everyone must be talked, cajoled, threatened, persuaded, argued, flattered, and shunted into a common mind. Nobody must be left out to be a prey to their own ideas and convictions. These, of course, are the principles of group dynamics, so beloved of the Marxists and the ecumenists. Evangelicals themselves are caught in the toils of this machinery, and often cannot see that it condemns them to impotence and ineffectiveness, which is precisely its purpose. Nothing must happen apart from the group, or that alienates from the group.

My friends, we must shake ourselves free from this system, or we shall do nothing at all. We are not called to seek a consensus, but to obey an imperative. We have to face facts. We cannot be in agreement with everybody. We cannot work with those whose aims are opposed to ours. We cannot go with those who are going in a different direction from ourselves. Division and separation are inescapable facts of the real world. We cannot work with those whose principles and aims are different from our own. Our Saviour faced that question and answered it with the words, 'He that is not with me is against me, and he that gathereth not with me scattereth abroad'. We can arrive at no other answer. It is impossible to work with everyone, and there is no point in trying, unless we are at least agreed about the direction in which we must go. Our business, and our aim, is to seek the reinstatement of the Reformation in the life of our national church.

Now it goes without saying, that there are those to whom that object is *anathema*. They are going in the very opposite direction. They make it abundantly clear what they are doing. We cannot, therefore, work with those who are looking to Rome, or with those who are already there. Catholicism in all its forms is the antithesis and contradiction of evangelical religion. They are like oil and water, they will not mix. Let me show you what I mean.

In his book, *Light from Old Times*, J. C. Ryle asks the question, 'Why were our Reformers burned?' He answers it by showing that in every case the question of their life or death turned upon their belief or disbelief in the *real presence*. 'Did they, or did they not, believe that the body and blood of Christ were really, that is, corporally, literally, locally, and materially present under the forms of bread and wine after the words of consecration were pronounced? Did they or did they not believe that the real body of Christ, which was born of the Virgin Mary, was present on the so-called altar so soon as the mystical words had passed the lips of the priest? Did they or did they not? That was the simple question. If they did not believe and admit it, they were burned.'

Why was this question so important and central to Papists and Protestants alike? Was it a mere logomachy, a strife about words? That is how many view it today. But it was not. The truth is that it was one of those points in which the total difference between Catholic and evangelical religion is focussed, so that acceptance or rejection of that one matter entails either acceptance or rejection of the whole system of Catholic religion. The mighty oak is, in a sense, contained in the acorn. All its ramifications, its branches, leaves, bark and roots, are latent and implicit in that small seed. Its development from this is a necessary and natural consequence. And so with the doctrine of the *real presence*. It contains the germ of Catholic religion, and all the manifestations and implications of it can be developed from it with a perfectly logical consistency. The *real presence* in the elements presupposes the power of the priest to make it so. The power of the priest is confined to the so-called apostolic succession and the validity of his orders, viz., that he was ordained with the intention of making him a sacrificing priest. The essence of priestly power is that the grace of forgiveness and reconciliation is only communicated through the priestly office, and through the valid celebration of the sacraments. Without the grace of baptism, penance, and the mass, the individual cannot be saved, for he cannot do any good works that merit salvation. Without priestly mediation the benefits of the death of Christ are not available. This is the nature of Catholic religion – grace tied to an order of men. Once you admit and believe in the real presence of Christ in the sacrament all this follows as night follows day – all this which is the antithesis of evangelical religion.

Our Reformers knew what they were about. It was no strife of words. No man would throw his life away for that. Cranmer, therefore, spoke plainly for them all when he said, 'They [the Papists] say that Christ is corporally under, or in, the form of bread and wine. We say that Christ is not there, neither corporally nor spiritually; but in them that worthily eat and drink the bread and wine he is spiritually and corporally in heaven'. There he showed the difference between evangelical religion and Catholicism. He made it clear that he was not going their way at all, but in the very opposite direction. Christ is present in the hearts of his people, not in the bread and wine. Despite all the talk about 'agreed statements' on the eucharist and other subjects, you will never get a Roman Catholic, or an Anglo-catholic, to agree with that, for the simple reason that it strikes at the very root of the priestly system of religion. Likewise you will never get a Roman Catholic or Anglo-catholic to agree to the doctrine of justification by the imputed righteousness of Christ, for that similarly has the effect of destroying the system of Catholic religion.

So what we are dealing with in Catholicism is not just another facet of Christian truth, but the very antithesis of evangelical religion. They are not travelling the same way, and so it is a waste of time talking about going with them. I noticed recently what appeared to be a Freudian slip of the tongue when a Vatican spokesman was arranging the Papal tour of Eire. He spoke of the non-christian religions, by which he meant Anglicans, Methodists, and Presbyterians.

What then of Liberals and Radicals? Can we go with them? We don't want to be accused of sharing the sympathies of a nineteenth century Bishop of St. David's, who in his paper on 'Proofs of the Inspiration of the Sibylline Verses', read at a meeting of the Royal Society of Literature, said, 'at all events a pagan is not a Papist'. Radicals and Liberals may not be Roman Catholics, but are they going the same way as ourselves?

Much of the stridency of self-confidence has gone out of Liberalism in recent years. We do not hear much today about the 'assured result of modern scholarship' for the simple reason that modern scholarship is no longer assured about anything. We have entered the age of agnosticism in theology. We cannot, it is said, really be sure about anything. We must preserve a reverent silence, for our insights are only partial and our knowledge relative. This is the significance of the report of the Archbishops' Commission on Doctrine entitled, *Christian Believing.* It is, in fact, anything but that. The past, it states, is largely inaccessible. We cannot really be sure about anything in the Bible. The authors of the report are adrift on a sea of cultural relativism with no horizon within sight. This is specially true of the chairman of the commission, and editor of the report, Maurice Wiles. I heard him say once, at Lincoln, that we cannot be sure about the Trinity, or about the divinity of our Lord, or any of these important doctrines. We can say nothing with certainty about these matters. It reminds me of the dictum of Ludwig Wittgenstein, with which he concluded his *Tractatus,* 'Whereof we cannot speak, thereof we must be silent'. But the trouble with these people is they keep on talking, and writing books too!

There are, of course, other signs. Who would have thought that the author of *Honest to God* would, twelve years later, write a book entitled *Redating the New Testament* in which he overthrows all the Liberal assumptions about the New Testament, and suggests what only the most conservative scholars would formerly have suggested, viz., that all the books of the New Testament were written within forty years of the crucifixion? The fact of the matter is that the mood of scepticism and uncertainty has created a theological vacuum now in the church in which all sorts of things can happen. We may find men beginning to move in a more conservative direction. We may begin to find that some of them are walking along the same way as ourselves. If we find that is so, we should welcome it, but we will not deviate from our path, because we know where we are going. Bunyan's Pilgrim encountered many sorts of people on his journey, Mr. Worldly-Wiseman, Mr. Talkative, Mr. Ignorance, Mr. By-Ends, to name but a few. He walked and talked with them, but only so far as they were going his way. We will not discourage any from going our way, but we will not change our course or slacken our pace for them.

And what of our relations with men of Reformed beliefs in other denominations. We deeply regret the rift that has taken place in recent years between Anglican evangelicals and Non-conformist evangelicals. It ought not to be. It had led some of our brethren in the Free Churches to ask not, 'Can any good thing come out of the Church of England?' but, 'Can any good thing remain in the Church of England?' We are sorry that they think this of us. We want them to understand that we are in the Church of England for a reason. We are in it to make it once more a Reformed church, where the doctrines of the Reformation are honoured and taught. We have a work to do which is barely begun, but we shall do it, by God's grace, and in the meantime we would wish our relations to be of the most cordial and sympathetic.

Now I come to the last of my questions: *What is our role as Anglican evangelicals to be?* I have already anticipated and answered this question to some extent. Our objective is the reinstatement of the English Reformation, its teaching and principles, in the life of the Church of England. But our role is something wider than that. It concerns what we must do in order to bring that about. How are we to act? What part must we play in order to achieve that end?

As I see it, the role of evangelicals in the Church of England is to be witnesses to the truth.

First, we must bear witness to the doctrines of the Reformation, which are the teachings of Scripture. We can make our appeal to the Bible. We can show these great teachings are based upon the Bible. The truth has a moral and spiritual force. The truth is mighty and will prevail. It cannot be trodden down and dismissed. But the truth needs witnesses. What greater vocation can we have than to follow him who said, 'For this cause came I into the world, that I should bear witness to the truth. Everyone that is of the truth heareth my voice'? We must make our appeal to the consciences of men. Those who are of the truth will listen. They are waiting for us to speak!

Secondly, we must witness to the true faith of the Church of England. What we are speaking about is not new, it is of the essence of Anglicanism. We want to see a renascence of true Anglicanism. Let no one accuse us of disloyalty or extremism. We want what was and has been central to the Church of England brought back into the centre. Our church has been suffering for more than a hundred years from self-induced amnesia, from forgetfulness of its real past and true identity. It has been living in never-never-land. We want it to recover its identity and, with it, a sense of purpose. We want it to recover its true teaching and, with it, the message of the Gospel that the nation needs. And to these things we must be witnesses.

And, lastly, we must be witnesses to the dealings of God with our nation. The Reformation left an indelible mark upon our church and nation. It was the providential dealing of God with us as a people. He gave us His Word, He gave us men of God to expound it, He gave us faithful witnesses, 'whereby we have been brought out of darkness and error into the clear light and true knowledge of Him and His Son Jesus Christ'. We did not merit any of this. He dealt with us in a special and significant way. We cannot turn our backs upon our history, and we dare not deny the providences of God to our nation. Our attempts to do so have resulted in our shame. It is time to start afresh, to begin a new page in our history.

It is time to repent, not of the Reformation, but of our neglect and denial of it. The genius and spirit of our church and nation are bound up with God's dealings with us at that time, and our spirits can only be set free by the free acceptance of what we are, and what God has made us to be.

The role of evangelicals, therefore, in the Church of England is to be witnesses to these things. The word 'witness' transliterated from the Greek is 'martyr'. There was no lack of witnesses four hundred years ago when the fires of persecution burned in this land. Nearly three hundred perished in the flames. We live in easier times, and are called upon to witness with our lives, not by our deaths. Surely we can do that. It is as vital that witnesses be found now as then. We must not fail our generation, nor can we fail to heed the Divine Imperative that lays this responsibility upon us.

Printed by F. & P. Piggott Ltd.
Round Church Street,
Cambridge